BUSINESS MARKETING

By Author

Andleeb Kamal

Gyanvriksha Publication

Gyanvriksha Publication

ज्ञानोद्याने, पुस्तकं सर्वं बीजम्

Gyanvriksha Publications

Email: gyanvrikshapublications@gmail.com

First Edition - 2024

Disclaimer

The content of this book, "Business Marketing" by Andleeb Kamal, is intended for educational and informational purposes only. While every effort has been made to ensure the accuracy and reliability of the information presented, the author and publisher make no warranties or representations regarding the completeness, accuracy, or applicability of the content in specific business contexts.

Readers are advised to consult with qualified professionals and conduct their research before making any business, financial, or marketing decisions based on the information provided in this book. The strategies and insights discussed herein are meant to serve as a general guide and may not be suitable for every situation.

Neither the author nor Gyanvriksha Publications shall be held liable for any damages, losses, or legal actions that may arise from the use or misuse of the information contained in this book. All opinions expressed are those of the author and do not necessarily reflect the views of Gyanvriksha Publications.

This book may include references to third-party products, services, or organizations. Such references are for illustrative purposes only and

Acknowledgement

Writing a book is a collaborative effort, and I am deeply grateful for the support and encouragement I have received throughout this journey.

First and foremost, I want to thank my family and friends for their unwavering support and understanding. Your encouragement and belief in my work have inspired and motivated me.

I would also like to thank my colleagues and mentors who have provided valuable insights and feedback. Your expertise and guidance have been instrumental in shaping the content of this book.

A special thanks to the team at Gyanvriksha Publications for their professionalism and dedication in bringing this book to life. Your support has been crucial in ensuring that this project reaches its full potential.

Finally, I want to acknowledge all the marketing professionals and students who continue to push the boundaries of this field. Your passion and innovation drive the future of marketing and inspire others to strive for excellence.

Thank you all for being a part of this journey.

About the Author

Andleeb Kamal grew up in the lively and culturally rich region of UP West, where her curiosity and creativity began to take root early on. Even as a child, she found herself captivated by the mysteries of rocket science and the imaginative world of advertisements that we encounter every day. These twin fascinations—science and creativity—have shaped her journey in profound ways.

When it came time to choose a path for her higher education, Andleeb knew she wanted to blend her interests in a way that felt true to her. She enrolled at Teerthanker Mahaveer University in Moradabad, Uttar Pradesh, where she pursued a Bachelor of Business Administration, specializing in Brand Management and Communication. It was here that she began to understand the power of storytelling in business, how a brand could speak to people's hearts and minds.

Then, the pandemic hit, turning the world upside down. But instead of letting the challenges overwhelm her, Andleeb saw this as an opportunity to grow. With much of her education shifting online, she found herself with extra time—time she decided to invest in herself. She completed a course in Digital Marketing, expanding her understanding of how the digital world connects people. And because she never settles for the ordinary, she also pursued a postgraduate diploma in Travel and Tourism from Jamia Millia Islamia, a top-ranked central university. Juggling all this while working with Ivory Publication showcased her incredible ability to multitask and remain focused on her goals.

Today, Andleeb is furthering her education with an Executive MBA at Jamia Millia Islamia in New Delhi. But her story isn't just about academic and professional accomplishments. From a young age, writing has been her sanctuary, a place where she can pour out her thoughts and emotions. What started as a way to cope with the complexities of life has blossomed into a passion for poetry and storytelling. Andleeb's poems and micro tales aren't just creative expressions—they're pieces of her heart, fragments of her experiences, and reflections of her soul.

For Andleeb, writing is more than just putting words on paper; it's about sharing a piece of herself with the world. It's about connecting with others on a level that goes beyond everyday conversations. Her writing often carries the weight of her dreams, her hopes, and the lessons learned from her struggles. She dreams of reaching great heights, not just for herself but for others, too. Through her work with Ink Freedom Publication, she hopes to create a space where people can freely express their creativity and explore the depths of their imagination.

Andleeb Kamal's journey is a testament to the power of resilience, passion, and the courage to follow one's dreams. She's not just a student or a professional—she's a storyteller, a dreamer, and a creator. As she continues to write her own story, she invites others to do the same, to find their voice and share it with the world.

Prologue

Welcome to "Business Marketing." In a world where the marketplace is increasingly crowded and competitive, understanding the principles of marketing is not just beneficial—it's essential. This book aims to provide a comprehensive exploration of business marketing, blending theoretical insights with practical applications to help you navigate the complex landscape of modern marketing.

As businesses strive to connect with consumers and differentiate themselves from competitors, marketing strategies have evolved rapidly. From the rise of digital platforms to the increasing emphasis on data-driven decisions, marketers face a dynamic environment where adaptability and innovation are key. This book will guide you through these changes, offering tools and strategies to enhance your marketing efforts and achieve your business goals.

Our journey together will explore fundamental concepts, delve into real-world case studies, and uncover the latest trends shaping the future of marketing. Whether you're a seasoned marketer or new to the field, this book will provide valuable insights to help you succeed in the ever-evolving world of business marketing.

Preface

The landscape of business marketing is ever-changing, driven by technological advancements, evolving consumer behaviours, and shifting market dynamics. As an experienced marketer, I have witnessed firsthand the transformative power of effective marketing strategies and the challenges that come with navigating this complex field.

In writing "Business Marketing," my goal is to distil my years of experience into a resource that is both informative and practical. This book is designed to bridge the gap between theoretical knowledge and real-world application, offering actionable insights that can be applied to a variety of business contexts.

Throughout this book, you will find a blend of foundational concepts and cutting-edge strategies. Each chapter is crafted to build your understanding progressively, from the basics of market research to advanced topics like distribution channels and marketing metrics. I hope that this book serves as a valuable guide in your marketing journey, equipping you with the knowledge and skills needed to excel in today's competitive market.

Thank you for embarking on this journey with me. I am excited to share my insights and help you navigate the dynamic world of business marketing.

Contents

Chapter 1: Introduction to Business Marketing

Welcome to the exciting world of business marketing! As we embark on this journey together, think of this chapter as your gateway into understanding how businesses connect with their customers, build their brands, and ultimately, drive their success. Whether you're new to marketing or looking to refresh your knowledge, this chapter will provide a solid foundation for the concepts you'll encounter throughout the book.

Understanding Business Marketing

At its core, business marketing is about creating, communicating, and delivering value to customers. It’s not just about selling products or services; it's about building relationships and meeting the needs of your target audience. Marketing helps businesses understand what customers want, how they want it, and at what price. It's a dynamic field that involves strategic planning, creative thinking, and a deep understanding of human behavior.

The Importance of Marketing in Business

Marketing plays a crucial role in the success of any business. It’s the bridge between a company and its customers, and it's vital for several reasons:

1. **Customer Connection:** Marketing helps businesses understand and connect with their target audience. By identifying customer needs and preferences, companies can tailor their offerings to meet those demands effectively.
2. **Brand Building:** Effective marketing establishes and strengthens a brand's identity. It helps create a positive perception of the company in the minds of customers, which can lead to increased brand loyalty and repeat business.
3. **Competitive Advantage:** In a crowded marketplace, marketing strategies can differentiate a business from its competitors. Unique selling propositions, innovative campaigns, and strong brand messaging can give a company an edge over its rivals.
4. **Revenue Generation:** Ultimately, marketing drives sales. Through various channels such as advertising, promotions, and digital marketing, businesses can attract potential customers and convert them into loyal clients.

Key Concepts and Terminology

To navigate the world of business marketing, it's essential to be familiar with some key concepts and terminology:

- **Market Research:** The process of gathering and analyzing information about consumers' needs and preferences. It helps businesses make informed decisions about their products, services, and marketing strategies.
- **Target Market:** A specific group of consumers that a company aims to reach with its products or services. Understanding the target market is crucial for developing effective marketing campaigns.
- **Marketing Mix (4 Ps):** The combination of Product, Price, Place, and Promotion that a company uses to market its offerings. Balancing these elements is key to a successful marketing strategy.
- **Branding:** The process of creating a unique name, symbol, or design that identifies and differentiates a product or company from others. Branding helps build customer loyalty and trust.
- **Customer Value:** The perception of what a product or service is worth to a customer compared to the alternatives. Providing

value is essential for attracting and retaining customers.

How Business Marketing Has Evolved

Marketing has come a long way from traditional methods like print advertising and direct mail. The digital age has transformed the landscape, bringing new opportunities and challenges. Today, businesses leverage online platforms, social media, and data analytics to reach and engage with customers. The rise of digital marketing has made it possible to target audiences more precisely and measure the effectiveness of marketing efforts in real-time.

Key Takeaways

1. **Marketing is Relationship-Driven:** Successful marketing is about building and maintaining strong relationships with customers. It's not just about making a sale but about creating a positive experience that encourages customer loyalty.

2. **Adaptability is Crucial:** The marketing landscape is constantly changing. Staying updated with the latest trends and technologies is essential for staying competitive and meeting the evolving needs of consumers.

3. **Data-Driven Decisions:** In today's digital world, data plays a significant role in

shaping marketing strategies. Analyzing customer data helps businesses make informed decisions and optimize their marketing efforts.

Additional Points

- **The Role of Creativity:** Creativity is at the heart of effective marketing. Innovative ideas and compelling storytelling can capture attention and leave a lasting impression on customers.
- **Ethical Considerations:** Marketing should be conducted with integrity and honesty. Ethical practices build trust with customers and contribute to a positive brand reputation.
- **Continuous Learning:** Marketing is a dynamic field with constant changes. Engaging in continuous learning and professional development is essential for staying ahead and refining your skills.

In conclusion, business marketing is a multifaceted discipline that combines strategy, creativity, and a deep understanding of consumer behavior. As you progress through this book, keep in mind that successful marketing is not just about selling a product but about creating value and building lasting relationships with your customers. Let's dive deeper into each aspect of business marketing in the following chapters and discover how to harness its power to drive business success.

Chapter 2: Market Research and Analysis

Welcome to Chapter 2, where we delve into the fascinating world of market research and analysis. This chapter is designed to equip you with the tools and knowledge necessary to understand and implement effective market research strategies. Think of market research as the compass that guides your marketing efforts—without it, navigating the market can be challenging and uncertain.

The Role of Market Research

Market research is the process of collecting, analyzing, and interpreting data about a market, including information about the target audience, competitors, and the overall industry. Its primary role is to provide businesses with valuable insights that inform decision-making and strategy development. Here's why market research is crucial:

1. **Informed Decision-Making:** Market research helps businesses make informed decisions by providing data-driven insights. Whether you're launching a new product, entering a new market, or adjusting your marketing strategy, research offers a solid foundation for your choices.

2. **Understanding Customer Needs:** By identifying customer preferences, needs, and behaviors, market research helps businesses tailor their products and services to better meet customer expectations. This understanding leads to improved customer satisfaction and loyalty.
3. **Identifying Opportunities and Threats:** Research uncovers potential opportunities for growth and highlights possible threats from competitors or market changes. This proactive approach enables businesses to adapt and stay ahead of the curve.
4. **Minimizing Risks:** Conducting thorough market research helps reduce risks associated with business decisions. It provides insights into market demand, competitive landscape, and potential challenges, allowing businesses to mitigate risks effectively.

Methods for Conducting Market Research

Market research can be conducted using various methods, each offering unique insights. Here are some commonly used methods:

1. **Surveys and Questionnaires:** These are among the most popular methods for gathering data directly from consumers.

Surveys can be administered online, via phone, or in person. They help collect quantitative data on customer preferences, satisfaction, and purchasing behavior.

2. **Interviews:** In-depth interviews with individuals or focus groups provide qualitative insights into customer attitudes, motivations, and experiences. This method is useful for understanding the underlying reasons behind customer behaviors and opinions.
3. **Observation:** Observational research involves watching and recording consumer behavior in natural settings. This method can reveal how customers interact with products or services and identify areas for improvement.
4. **Secondary Research:** This involves analyzing existing data from sources such as industry reports, academic studies, and market research firms. Secondary research is valuable for gaining a broader understanding of market trends and competitive dynamics.
5. **Experiments:** Experimental research involves testing different variables to see how they affect consumer behavior. For example, a business might test different

pricing strategies or promotional offers to determine their impact on sales.

Analyzing Market Trends and Data

Once you've collected data through various research methods, the next step is to analyze it to extract meaningful insights. Here's how to approach data analysis:

1. **Data Organization:** Start by organizing the data you've collected. This may involve categorizing responses, cleaning up any inconsistencies, and preparing the data for analysis. Tools like spreadsheets and data analysis software can help with this process.
2. **Identify Patterns and Trends:** Look for patterns and trends in the data. This might include changes in customer preferences, emerging market segments, or shifts in buying behavior. Identifying these trends helps in forecasting future market conditions and making strategic decisions.
3. **Segmentation:** Break down the data into different segments based on variables such as demographics, geography, or purchasing behavior. Segmentation allows you to tailor marketing strategies to specific groups, making them more effective.

4. **Competitive Analysis:** Compare your findings with information about competitors. Understanding how your business stacks up against others in the market can reveal areas of strength and opportunities for improvement.
5. **Draw Conclusions:** Based on your analysis, draw conclusions about the market and your target audience. These conclusions should inform your marketing strategy, product development, and other business decisions.

Additional Points

- **The Importance of Continuous Research:** Market research is not a one-time activity but an ongoing process. Continually gathering and analyzing data helps businesses stay current with market trends and adapt to changes effectively.
- **Utilizing Technology:** Leveraging technology, such as data analytics tools and customer relationship management (CRM) systems, can enhance the accuracy and efficiency of market research. These tools provide advanced analytics and real-time insights.
- **Ethical Considerations:** Ensure that your research practices are ethical and respect

the privacy of participants. Adhering to ethical standards builds trust with consumers and enhances the credibility of your research findings.

- **Actionable Insights:** The ultimate goal of market research is to generate actionable insights that drive decision-making. Focus on translating research findings into practical strategies and solutions that benefit your business.

In summary, market research and analysis are essential components of a successful marketing strategy. By understanding your market, customers, and competitors, you can make informed decisions that lead to business growth and success. As we continue to explore various aspects of business marketing, remember that effective research is the key to unlocking valuable insights and staying ahead in a competitive landscape.

Chapter 3: Consumer Behavior

Welcome to Chapter 3, where we explore the fascinating field of consumer behavior. Understanding how consumers think, feel, and act is crucial for crafting effective marketing strategies. This chapter will provide insights into consumer needs and wants, the psychological and social factors influencing buying decisions, and how to segment and target markets effectively.

Understanding Consumer Needs and Wants

To effectively market your products or services, it's essential to grasp what drives consumer behavior. Consumers have both needs and wants that shape their purchasing decisions:

1. **Needs vs. Wants:** Needs are basic requirements for survival, such as food, water, and shelter. Wants, on the other hand, are desires that go beyond the basic necessities. For example, a need might be a car for transportation, while a want could be a luxury sports car for personal enjoyment.
2. **The Hierarchy of Needs:** Abraham Maslow's Hierarchy of Needs is a useful framework for understanding consumer motivations. This model suggests that

people are motivated to fulfill basic needs (like physiological and safety needs) before moving on to higher-level needs (such as social belonging, esteem, and self-actualization). Marketing strategies can be tailored to address these varying levels of needs.

3. **Consumer Decision-Making Process:** Consumers go through a series of stages when making a purchase decision: problem recognition, information search, evaluation of alternatives, purchase decision, and post-purchase behavior. Understanding this process helps businesses address potential concerns and influence decision-making at each stage.

Psychological and Social Influences on Buying Decisions

Consumer behavior is influenced by a complex interplay of psychological and social factors. Let's break these down:

1. **Psychological Factors:**
    - **Perception:** How consumers perceive a product or brand affects their buying decisions. Perception is influenced by past experiences, beliefs, and attitudes. For example, a

brand perceived as high-quality will likely attract more customers.

- **Motivation:** Motivation drives consumers to act. It can be intrinsic (internal satisfaction) or extrinsic (external rewards). Understanding what motivates your target audience can help tailor your marketing messages.
- **Learning:** Consumers learn from their experiences, which can shape future behavior. Positive experiences with a brand can lead to repeat purchases, while negative experiences might deter future engagement.
- **Attitudes and Beliefs:** Consumers' attitudes and beliefs towards products or brands play a significant role in their decisions. Positive attitudes can encourage purchase, while negative attitudes may act as barriers.

2. **Social Factors:**

   - **Family:** Family members influence each other's buying decisions. For example, parents might influence the choice of products for their children, while family preferences can shape household purchasing behavior.

- **Reference Groups:** Consumers are influenced by groups they belong to or aspire to join, such as friends, colleagues, or social influencers. These groups can impact brand perception and purchasing choices.
- **Social Class:** A consumer's social class, which is often determined by factors such as income, education, and occupation, affects their buying behavior and preferences. Marketing strategies can be customized to appeal to different social classes.

Market Segmentation and Targeting

Once you understand consumer behavior, the next step is to segment the market and target specific groups effectively. Here's how:

1. **Market Segmentation:** This involves dividing the market into distinct groups of consumers with similar characteristics or needs. Common bases for segmentation include:
   - **Demographic Segmentation:** Dividing the market based on age,

gender, income, education, or occupation.

- **Geographic Segmentation:** Segmenting based on location, such as region, city, or climate.
- **Psychographic Segmentation:** Classifying consumers based on lifestyle, values, interests, and personality traits.
- **Behavioral Segmentation:** Grouping consumers based on their behavior, such as purchasing habits, brand loyalty, and product usage.

2. **Targeting:** After segmentation, businesses need to select the most appropriate target market. This involves evaluating each segment's attractiveness and deciding which segments to focus on. Targeting strategies include:

   - **Undifferentiated Targeting:** Offering a single product to the entire market, suitable for products with universal appeal.
   - **Differentiated Targeting:** Creating different marketing mixes for different segments, ideal for businesses with diverse product lines.

- **Concentrated Targeting:** Focusing on a single market segment, useful for niche markets where specialized offerings are needed.
- **Micromarketing:** Tailoring products and marketing efforts to individual customers or local segments, often enabled by advanced data analytics.

Additional Points

- **Customer Journey Mapping:** Understanding the customer journey—the entire experience from awareness to post-purchase—can provide deeper insights into consumer behavior and help refine marketing strategies.
- **Emotional Influences:** Emotions play a significant role in consumer decision-making. Crafting emotionally resonant marketing messages can strengthen brand connections and influence buying behavior.
- **Cultural Influences:** Cultural background can impact consumer preferences and behavior. Considering cultural differences and norms in your marketing strategy can enhance relevance and appeal.
- **Ethical Marketing:** Respecting consumer privacy and avoiding manipulative practices is essential. Ethical marketing

fosters trust and long-term customer relationships.

In summary, understanding consumer behavior is crucial for developing effective marketing strategies. By analyzing consumer needs and wants, considering psychological and social influences, and implementing market segmentation and targeting, you can create marketing campaigns that resonate with your audience and drive business success. As we move forward, keep these insights in mind to build a solid foundation for your marketing efforts.

Chapter 4: Marketing Strategies and Planning

Welcome to Chapter 4, where we dive into the art and science of developing marketing strategies and planning. Think of this chapter as your roadmap to creating effective marketing campaigns that drive business growth and success. By the end of this chapter, you'll be equipped with the knowledge to develop a strategic marketing approach, set clear objectives, and craft a comprehensive marketing plan.

Developing a Marketing Strategy

Creating a successful marketing strategy involves understanding your business goals, analyzing the market environment, and defining how you'll achieve your objectives. Here's how to approach it:

1. **Understand Your Business Goals:** Your marketing strategy should align with your overall business objectives. Start by identifying what your business aims to achieve—whether it's increasing sales, entering new markets, or enhancing brand awareness.
2. **Conduct a SWOT Analysis:** A SWOT analysis (Strengths, Weaknesses, Opportunities,

Threats) helps you understand your business's internal strengths and weaknesses, as well as external opportunities and threats. This analysis provides a foundation for developing a strategy that leverages strengths and opportunities while addressing weaknesses and threats.

3. **Define Your Target Audience:** Knowing your target audience is crucial for tailoring your marketing strategy. Use insights from market research to define who your ideal customers are, what they need, and how they prefer to be reached.

4. **Position Your Brand:** Positioning is about how you want your brand to be perceived in the market. Develop a unique value proposition that differentiates your brand from competitors and resonates with your target audience.

5. **Select Marketing Channels:** Choose the most effective channels for reaching your audience. This might include digital channels (such as social media, email, and content marketing), traditional channels (like print ads and events), or a mix of both.

6. **Allocate Resources:** Determine how much budget, time, and manpower you can invest

in your marketing efforts. Allocate resources based on the channels and tactics that will yield the best results.

Setting Marketing Objectives

Clear, actionable objectives are essential for guiding your marketing efforts and measuring success. Here's how to set effective marketing objectives:

1. **SMART Objectives:** Ensure your objectives are Specific, Measurable, Achievable, Relevant, and Time-bound. For example, instead of saying "Increase sales," a SMART objective would be "Increase sales by 20% over the next six months through an online advertising campaign."
2. **Align with Business Goals:** Your marketing objectives should support your overall business goals. If your business aims to expand into new markets, a marketing objective might be "Achieve a 15% market share in the new region within the next year."
3. **Focus on Key Metrics:** Identify the key performance indicators (KPIs) that will help you measure progress towards your objectives. Common KPIs include sales revenue, website traffic, conversion rates, and customer acquisition costs.

4. **Prioritize Objectives:** Determine which objectives are most critical to your business's success and prioritize them. This helps focus your efforts and resources on what matters most.

Crafting a Marketing Plan

A well-crafted marketing plan outlines how you'll implement your strategy and achieve your objectives. Here's a step-by-step guide to creating your marketing plan:

1. **Executive Summary:** Start with an overview of your marketing strategy, objectives, and key tactics. This summary provides a snapshot of what's to come and aligns everyone involved in the plan.
2. **Market Analysis:** Include a detailed analysis of your target market, including customer demographics, market trends, and competitive landscape. This section helps contextualize your marketing efforts within the broader market environment.
3. **Marketing Strategy:** Detail your strategic approach, including your positioning, value proposition, and key messages. Outline how you'll leverage different marketing channels to reach your target audience.

4. **Action Plan:** Break down your strategy into actionable steps. Specify the tasks, timelines, and responsibilities for each marketing activity. For example, if you're launching a social media campaign, outline the content calendar, platforms, and team members involved.
5. **Budget:** Allocate your budget across various marketing activities. Include estimates for advertising, promotions, content creation, and other expenses. Ensure your budget aligns with your objectives and expected return on investment.
6. **Evaluation and Control:** Define how you'll monitor and evaluate the effectiveness of your marketing efforts. Set up a system for tracking KPIs, analyzing performance data, and making adjustments as needed.

Additional Points

- **Flexibility and Adaptability:** While it's important to have a detailed plan, be prepared to adapt as needed. Market conditions, customer preferences, and business circumstances can change, so flexibility is key to staying on track.
- **Integration with Sales and Operations:** Ensure that your marketing plan is

integrated with your sales and operations strategies. Coordination between departments helps streamline efforts and achieve cohesive business objectives.

- **Continuous Improvement:** Regularly review and assess the effectiveness of your marketing plan. Gather feedback, analyze results, and make data-driven adjustments to continually improve your marketing efforts.
- **Stakeholder Involvement:** Involve key stakeholders in the planning process. This includes team members, partners, and even customers. Their input can provide valuable insights and foster buy-in for your marketing strategy.

In conclusion, developing a marketing strategy and crafting a marketing plan are essential steps for achieving business success. By understanding your business goals, setting clear objectives, and creating a detailed plan, you set the stage for effective marketing efforts that drive growth and build strong customer relationships. As we move forward, remember that a well-thought-out strategy and plan are the foundation for your marketing success.

Chapter 5: Product Management

Welcome to Chapter 5, where we dive into the essential aspects of product management. This chapter will cover the product development and life cycle, branding and positioning, and the critical elements of product differentiation and innovation. Understanding these concepts will equip you with the tools to manage products effectively and ensure they meet market needs and stand out from the competition.

Product Development and Life Cycle

Managing a product effectively begins with understanding its development and life cycle. This knowledge helps you navigate the various stages a product goes through from inception to decline.

1. **Product Development:** This phase involves turning an idea into a tangible product. Here's how to approach it:
    - **Idea Generation:** Start by brainstorming and generating ideas based on market research, customer needs, and industry trends. Encourage creativity and look for innovative solutions to existing problems.

- **Concept Development:** Develop a detailed concept that outlines the product's features, benefits, and target market. Create prototypes or models to visualize and test the idea.
- **Business Analysis:** Assess the feasibility of the product idea by conducting a business analysis. Evaluate costs, potential revenue, and profitability to determine if the product is viable.
- **Product Design and Development:** Refine the product design based on feedback and testing. Develop the final version of the product, ensuring it meets quality standards and customer expectations.
- **Market Testing:** Test the product in a limited market to gather feedback and identify any issues. Use this information to make necessary adjustments before a full-scale launch.

2. **Product Life Cycle (PLC):** Every product goes through a life cycle consisting of several stages:
    - **Introduction:** This is the stage where the product is launched into the

market. Marketing efforts focus on creating awareness and generating interest.

- **Growth:** During the growth stage, the product gains acceptance and sales increase. Focus on expanding market reach and differentiating the product from competitors.
- **Maturity:** In the maturity stage, sales growth slows as the product reaches market saturation. The focus shifts to maintaining market share and maximizing profitability.
- **Decline:** Eventually, the product may enter the decline stage, where sales decrease due to market saturation, changing consumer preferences, or technological advancements. Consider strategies for revitalizing the product or phasing it out.

Branding and Positioning

Branding and positioning are crucial for creating a strong market presence and differentiating your product from competitors. Here's how to approach these elements:

1. **Branding:** Branding involves creating a unique identity for your product or company. It includes:

- **Brand Identity:** Develop a strong brand identity that includes a name, logo, tagline, and visual elements. Your brand identity should reflect your product's values and resonate with your target audience.
- **Brand Equity:** Build brand equity by establishing a positive reputation and strong emotional connection with customers. This involves delivering consistent quality, exceptional customer service, and a compelling brand story.
- **Brand Personality:** Infuse your brand with a personality that aligns with your target audience's values and preferences. A brand personality helps create a relatable and memorable image.

2. **Positioning:** Positioning is about how you want your product to be perceived in the market. It involves:

    - **Unique Selling Proposition (USP):** Define your product's USP—what makes it unique and valuable to customers. Your USP should highlight the key benefits that set your product apart from competitors.

- **Positioning Statement:** Craft a clear and concise positioning statement that communicates the product's value and target audience. This statement should guide your marketing efforts and messaging.
- **Competitive Analysis:** Analyze your competitors to understand their positioning strategies. Identify gaps in the market and opportunities for positioning your product effectively.

Product Differentiation and Innovation

To stay competitive, it's essential to differentiate your product and foster innovation. Here's how to approach these aspects:

1. **Product Differentiation:** Differentiation involves making your product stand out from the competition. Consider the following strategies:
    - **Feature Differentiation:** Offer unique features or functionalities that address specific customer needs or problems.
    - **Quality Differentiation:** Ensure your product maintains high-quality standards that surpass those of competitors.

- **Design Differentiation:** Develop distinctive designs or packaging that make your product visually appealing and memorable.
- **Service Differentiation:** Provide exceptional customer service or support that enhances the overall product experience.

2. **Innovation:** Innovation is key to staying ahead in the market. Foster innovation by:
    - **Encouraging Creativity:** Create an environment that encourages brainstorming and creative problem-solving. Embrace new ideas and approaches to product development.
    - **Staying Informed:** Keep up with industry trends, technological advancements, and emerging customer needs. This knowledge helps identify opportunities for innovation.
    - **Investing in R&D:** Allocate resources to research and development (R&D) to explore new technologies, materials, and processes that can enhance your product.

Additional Points

- **Customer Feedback:** Continuously gather and analyze customer feedback to inform product improvements and innovations. Engaging with customers helps ensure that your product meets their evolving needs.
- **Sustainability:** Consider the environmental and social impact of your product. Incorporating sustainable practices and materials can enhance your brand's reputation and appeal to eco-conscious consumers.
- **Lifecycle Management:** Actively manage the product lifecycle by monitoring performance, adjusting strategies, and planning for future iterations or new product launches.
- **Cross-Functional Collaboration:** Collaborate with other departments, such as marketing, sales, and production, to ensure alignment and successful execution of product strategies.

In summary, effective product management involves understanding the product development process, establishing a strong brand and positioning, and fostering differentiation and innovation. By mastering these elements, you can manage products that resonate with customers, stand out in the market, and contribute to your business's success. As we move forward, keep these principles in mind to create and manage products that drive growth and create lasting value.

Chapter 6: Pricing Strategies

Welcome to Chapter 6, where we delve into the critical aspect of pricing strategies. Pricing isn't just about setting a number; it's a strategic decision that can impact your brand's position in the market, profitability, and overall business success. In this chapter, we'll explore the factors affecting pricing decisions, various pricing models and strategies, and how to implement effective pricing tactics.

Factors Affecting Pricing Decisions

Setting the right price for your product or service involves a careful analysis of several factors. Here's what you need to consider:

1. **Cost Structure:** Understanding your cost structure is fundamental. This includes both fixed costs (e.g., rent, salaries) and variable costs (e.g., materials, production). Your price must cover these costs and contribute to profitability. Calculate the break-even point—where total revenue equals total costs—to determine the minimum price needed to avoid losses.
2. **Market Demand:** Assess the demand for your product or service. Higher demand can justify a higher price, while lower demand might require a more competitive pricing approach. Conduct market research to

understand how much consumers are willing to pay and how demand fluctuates.

3. **Competitive Landscape:** Analyze your competitors' pricing strategies. Pricing too high might drive customers to competitors, while pricing too low could undermine your perceived value. Identify where your product fits in relation to competitors and set a price that reflects its value while remaining competitive.

4. **Customer Perception:** The price of your product influences how customers perceive its value. Premium pricing can suggest high quality, while lower pricing might appeal to budget-conscious consumers. Ensure your pricing aligns with your brand's image and the value proposition you offer.

5. **Market Positioning:** Your pricing should reflect your market positioning. If you're positioning your product as a luxury item, your pricing should reflect exclusivity. Conversely, if your aim is to be a cost leader, competitive pricing is essential.

6. **Economic Conditions:** External economic factors, such as inflation, interest rates, and economic downturns, can affect consumer purchasing power and demand. Adjust your pricing strategy to align with

current economic conditions and consumer spending behavior.

Pricing Models and Strategies

There are several pricing models and strategies you can use, each suited to different business objectives and market conditions. Here's an overview:

1. **Cost-Plus Pricing:** This model involves adding a markup to the cost of producing a product. It's straightforward—calculate the cost and add a percentage for profit. While easy to implement, it doesn't always account for market conditions or customer perception.

2. **Competitive Pricing:** Set prices based on what competitors are charging. This approach helps ensure you remain competitive but may not fully capture the unique value of your product. It's useful in highly competitive markets where price is a significant factor.

3. **Value-Based Pricing:** Set prices based on the perceived value to the customer rather than the cost. This strategy requires understanding how much value your product provides to consumers and setting a price that reflects that value. It's effective

for products that offer significant benefits or unique features.

4. **Penetration Pricing:** Introduce a product at a low price to attract customers and gain market share quickly. Once established, you can gradually raise the price. This strategy is useful for entering competitive markets but requires careful management to avoid long-term profitability issues.

5. **Skimming Pricing:** Set a high initial price to target early adopters and then lower it over time to attract a broader audience. This strategy maximizes revenue from different market segments. It's often used for innovative products with limited initial availability.

6. **Psychological Pricing:** Use pricing techniques that appeal to the psychological aspects of consumer behavior. For example, pricing something at $9.99 instead of $10.00 can make it seem like a better deal. This approach leverages consumer perception to drive sales.

7. **Bundle Pricing:** Offer multiple products or services together at a reduced price. Bundling can increase the perceived value and encourage customers to buy more. It's

effective for increasing average order value and clearing out inventory.

Implementing Effective Pricing Tactics

Once you've selected a pricing strategy, it's important to implement it effectively. Here's how to do that:

1. **Monitor and Adjust:** Regularly review your pricing strategy and make adjustments based on market conditions, cost changes, and consumer feedback. Pricing isn't static—be prepared to adapt as needed to stay competitive and meet business objectives.

2. **Communicate Value:** Clearly communicate the value of your product to justify your pricing. Use marketing messages, product descriptions, and promotional materials to highlight the benefits and features that justify the price.

3. **Test Pricing:** Conduct pricing tests to understand how different prices affect sales and customer behavior. A/B testing, where you compare two pricing options, can provide valuable insights into optimal pricing strategies.

4. **Use Discounts Strategically:** Offer discounts and promotions in a way that enhances sales without undermining your

pricing strategy. Limited-time offers, seasonal promotions, and loyalty discounts can attract customers and drive purchases.

5. **Educate Your Sales Team:** Ensure your sales team understands the pricing strategy and can effectively communicate it to customers. They should be able to explain the value proposition and handle pricing-related questions confidently.

Additional Points

- **Legal and Ethical Considerations:** Be aware of legal and ethical issues related to pricing, such as price fixing, predatory pricing, and price discrimination. Adhere to regulations and practices that promote fair competition and consumer trust.
- **Customer Segmentation:** Tailor pricing strategies to different customer segments based on their willingness to pay, needs, and preferences. This approach can maximize revenue and address diverse market segments effectively.
- **Pricing Tools and Software:** Utilize pricing tools and software to analyze data, manage pricing changes, and automate pricing decisions. These tools can provide insights and streamline pricing processes.

- **Global Pricing:** If operating in international markets, consider factors such as currency fluctuations, local economic conditions, and cultural differences in pricing strategies. Adapt your pricing approach to fit each market's specific context.

In conclusion, pricing strategies are a critical component of your marketing and business strategy. By understanding the factors that influence pricing decisions, choosing the right pricing model, and implementing effective tactics, you can set prices that drive profitability, meet customer expectations, and enhance your competitive position. As you move forward, remember that pricing is both an art and a science—continually refine your approach to achieve the best results for your business.

Chapter 7: Distribution Channels

Welcome to Chapter 7, where we explore the intricacies of distribution channels. Distribution channels are crucial for delivering your product or service to your customers effectively. They play a key role in ensuring that your product reaches the right audience in the right way. In this chapter, we will delve into understanding distribution networks, choosing the right distribution channels, and managing and optimizing distribution.

Understanding Distribution Networks

Distribution networks are the pathways through which products or services travel from the manufacturer to the end consumer. Understanding these networks is fundamental to ensuring efficient and effective distribution.

1. **Components of Distribution Networks:** A distribution network typically includes various intermediaries such as wholesalers, distributors, retailers, and agents. Each component plays a specific role in moving the product from the producer to the consumer:

- **Manufacturers:** The origin point of the product, where it is produced or assembled.
- **Wholesalers:** Intermediaries who purchase in bulk from manufacturers and sell to retailers or other businesses.
- **Distributors:** Entities that manage the logistics and distribution of products to retailers or end-users.
- **Retailers:** Businesses that sell products directly to consumers.
- **Agents and Brokers:** Individuals or firms that facilitate transactions between buyers and sellers, often taking a commission for their services.

2. **Distribution Network Design:** The design of your distribution network should align with your business goals, product type, and target market. Consider factors such as the geographical reach, the complexity of the supply chain, and the level of control you need over distribution.
3. **Channel Functions:** Distribution channels perform several key functions:

- **Transactional Functions:** Buying, selling, and taking ownership of products.
- **Logistical Functions:** Storing, transporting, and managing inventory.
- **Facilitating Functions:** Providing information, financing, and promotional support.

Choosing the Right Distribution Channels

Selecting the right distribution channels is critical to reaching your target market effectively and efficiently. Here's how to approach this decision:

1. **Direct vs. Indirect Channels:** Decide whether to use direct or indirect channels:
    - **Direct Channels:** Involve selling directly to consumers through your own sales force, website, or physical stores. This approach offers greater control over the customer experience and branding.
    - **Indirect Channels:** Involve intermediaries such as wholesalers and retailers. This approach can expand market reach and leverage

the expertise and resources of intermediaries.

2. **Channel Types:** Evaluate different types of distribution channels based on your product and market needs:
   - **Exclusive Distribution:** Limiting the number of outlets to maintain a high level of control and exclusivity. This is often used for luxury or high-end products.
   - **Selective Distribution:** Using a limited number of intermediaries to maintain a balance between control and market coverage. Suitable for products that require some level of expertise or service.
   - **Intensive Distribution:** Distributing products through as many outlets as possible to maximize reach and availability. This is common for everyday consumer goods.
3. **Channel Partners:** Choose partners that align with your brand values and business goals. Evaluate potential partners based on their market reach, reputation, and ability to handle your product effectively.
4. **Cost and Efficiency:** Consider the costs associated with each distribution channel

and the efficiency of delivering your product to the market. Balance the costs with the benefits of reaching your target audience and maintaining customer satisfaction.

Managing and Optimizing Distribution

Effective management and optimization of distribution channels are crucial for maintaining efficiency and meeting customer expectations. Here's how to approach this:

1. **Inventory Management:** Efficient inventory management ensures that products are available when and where needed. Implement inventory tracking systems to monitor stock levels, manage reorder points, and minimize stockouts or overstock situations.

2. **Logistics and Transportation:** Optimize logistics and transportation to reduce costs and improve delivery times. Evaluate shipping options, negotiate rates with carriers, and streamline logistics processes to enhance efficiency.

3. **Performance Monitoring:** Regularly assess the performance of your distribution channels. Use key performance indicators (KPIs) such as delivery accuracy, lead times, and customer satisfaction to

measure effectiveness and identify areas for improvement.

4. **Channel Coordination:** Ensure effective coordination between different channel partners. Establish clear communication channels, set expectations, and collaborate to address any issues or challenges that arise.

5. **Technology and Automation:** Leverage technology and automation to enhance distribution processes. Use software for inventory management, order processing, and data analytics to improve accuracy and efficiency.

Additional Points

- **Customer Feedback:** Gather feedback from customers regarding their experience with distribution and delivery. Use this information to make improvements and address any issues.

- **Flexibility and Adaptability:** Be prepared to adapt your distribution strategy based on changes in market conditions, customer preferences, or supply chain disruptions. Flexibility is key to maintaining an effective distribution network.

- **Sustainability Considerations:** Consider the environmental impact of your distribution practices. Implement sustainable practices such as reducing packaging waste, optimizing transportation routes, and exploring eco-friendly packaging options.

- **Global Distribution:** If operating internationally, consider factors such as local regulations, customs procedures, and cultural differences. Adapt your distribution strategy to fit the specific requirements of each international market.

In conclusion, effective distribution management is essential for delivering your product to the right place at the right time. By understanding distribution networks, choosing the right channels, and optimizing distribution processes, you can enhance efficiency, meet customer expectations, and achieve business success. As you move forward, remember that a well-managed distribution strategy is crucial for maintaining a competitive edge and ensuring that your products reach your customers effectively.

Chapter 8: Promotion and Advertising

Welcome to Chapter 8, where we dive into the dynamic world of promotion and advertising. Effective promotion and advertising are essential for communicating your product's value, attracting customers, and driving sales. In this chapter, we'll explore the role of promotion in marketing, the art of designing effective advertising campaigns, and the significance of digital marketing and social media in today's business landscape.

The Role of Promotion in Marketing

Promotion is a critical element of the marketing mix, encompassing various activities designed to inform, persuade, and remind customers about your product or service. It plays a pivotal role in shaping consumer perceptions and driving demand. Here's how promotion fits into the broader marketing strategy:

1. **Informing Customers:** Promotion helps inform potential customers about your product's features, benefits, and availability. This awareness is the first step in the buying process. For instance, promotional materials such as brochures, advertisements, and social media posts

provide essential information that guides customers in their decision-making.

2. **Persuading Customers:** Effective promotion persuades customers to choose your product over competitors. This involves highlighting unique selling points, demonstrating value, and addressing customer needs. Persuasive promotion can influence buying decisions and convert prospects into loyal customers.

3. **Reminding Customers:** After the initial purchase, promotion helps maintain customer interest and loyalty. Reminders about product benefits, updates, or special offers keep your brand top-of-mind and encourage repeat purchases. For example, email newsletters and loyalty programs are great ways to stay in touch with existing customers.

4. **Building Brand Image:** Promotion contributes to building and maintaining a positive brand image. Consistent messaging and branding across promotional channels help establish a strong, recognizable identity. This includes creating a cohesive look and feel in all advertising materials and communications.

Designing Effective Advertising Campaigns

Creating an advertising campaign involves a strategic approach to ensure it resonates with your target audience and achieves your marketing goals. Here's a step-by-step guide to designing effective advertising campaigns:

1. **Define Campaign Objectives:** Start by clearly defining what you want to achieve with your campaign. Objectives may include increasing brand awareness, driving website traffic, generating leads, or boosting sales. Setting specific, measurable goals helps you focus your efforts and measure success.

2. **Understand Your Audience:** Conduct thorough research to understand your target audience's demographics, interests, and behaviors. This knowledge allows you to tailor your messaging and choose the right channels to reach your audience effectively. Develop customer personas to guide your campaign strategy.

3. **Craft a Compelling Message:** Create a message that captures attention and communicates the core benefits of your product. Your message should be clear, engaging, and aligned with your brand's tone and voice. Focus on addressing customer pain points and highlighting how your product solves their problems.

4. **Choose the Right Media Channels:** Select media channels that are most effective for reaching your target audience. Options include television, radio, print media, online platforms, and social media. Consider the strengths and limitations of each channel and how they align with your campaign objectives.

5. **Design Creative Elements:** Develop creative elements such as visuals, copy, and call-to-action (CTA) that enhance your message and capture attention. Ensure that your design is visually appealing and aligns with your brand's identity. Test different creative approaches to determine what resonates best with your audience.

6. **Set a Budget:** Determine your advertising budget based on your campaign objectives and available resources. Allocate your budget across different media channels and creative elements. Monitor spending and adjust as needed to stay within budget while achieving desired results.

7. **Monitor and Evaluate Performance:** Track the performance of your advertising campaign using key performance indicators (KPIs) such as reach, engagement, conversion rates, and return on investment (ROI). Analyze the data to

assess the effectiveness of your campaign and identify areas for improvement.

Digital Marketing and Social Media

In today's digital age, digital marketing and social media play a crucial role in reaching and engaging with your audience. Here's how to leverage these platforms effectively:

1. **Digital Marketing Overview:** Digital marketing encompasses various online tactics, including search engine optimization (SEO), content marketing, email marketing, and pay-per-click (PPC) advertising. Each tactic has its unique benefits and can be used to complement traditional marketing efforts.
2. **Search Engine Optimization (SEO):** SEO involves optimizing your website and content to rank higher in search engine results. Use relevant keywords, create high-quality content, and improve website performance to enhance your visibility and attract organic traffic.
3. **Content Marketing:** Content marketing focuses on creating and sharing valuable content to engage your audience and build trust. This includes blog posts, articles, videos, infographics, and other types of

content that provide useful information and address customer needs.

4. **Email Marketing:** Email marketing involves sending targeted messages to your subscribers. Use email campaigns to promote special offers, share updates, and nurture leads. Personalize your emails and segment your audience to increase engagement and conversion rates.

5. **Pay-Per-Click (PPC) Advertising:** PPC advertising allows you to place ads on search engines and other platforms and pay only when someone clicks on your ad. It's an effective way to drive targeted traffic and generate leads quickly. Set clear goals and optimize your PPC campaigns for maximum ROI.

6. **Social Media Marketing:** Social media platforms such as Facebook, Instagram, Twitter, and LinkedIn offer opportunities to connect with your audience, share content, and run targeted ads. Develop a social media strategy that includes regular posting, engaging with followers, and utilizing paid advertising to reach a wider audience.

7. **Analytics and Insights:** Use analytics tools to track the performance of your digital

marketing and social media efforts. Monitor metrics such as website traffic, social media engagement, and conversion rates to evaluate success and make data-driven decisions.

Additional Points

- **Integrated Marketing Communication:** Ensure that your promotional efforts are integrated across all channels for a consistent brand message. This approach reinforces your message and enhances overall effectiveness.
- **Customer Engagement:** Focus on engaging with customers through interactive content, polls, contests, and personalized communication. Building relationships with customers fosters loyalty and encourages word-of-mouth promotion.
- **Trends and Innovations:** Stay updated with the latest trends and innovations in promotion and advertising. Emerging technologies, new platforms, and changing consumer behaviors can provide opportunities for creative and effective campaigns.
- **Legal and Ethical Considerations:** Adhere to legal and ethical guidelines in your advertising practices. Ensure transparency,

avoid misleading claims, and respect privacy regulations to build trust and maintain credibility.

In summary, effective promotion and advertising are essential for reaching your audience, building brand awareness, and driving sales. By understanding the role of promotion, designing impactful advertising campaigns, and leveraging digital marketing and social media, you can create compelling strategies that resonate with your target audience and achieve your marketing goals. As you move forward, remember that a well-rounded approach to promotion and advertising will help you stand out in a competitive market and foster lasting connections with your customers.

Chapter 9: Sales Management

Welcome to Chapter 9, where we delve into the essential aspects of sales management. Sales management is a critical function that directly impacts a company's revenue and growth. This chapter will guide you through building a sales strategy, mastering sales techniques and skills, and effectively managing sales teams and performance.

Building a Sales Strategy

A well-defined sales strategy provides direction and focus for your sales efforts. It outlines how your sales team will achieve its goals and align with your overall business objectives. Here's how to build an effective sales strategy:

1. **Understand Your Market:** Start by conducting a thorough analysis of your market. This includes understanding your target customers, market trends, and competitive landscape. Identify customer needs, preferences, and pain points to tailor your sales approach accordingly.

2. **Set Clear Objectives:** Define specific, measurable, achievable, relevant, and time-bound (SMART) objectives for your sales team. These objectives might include

revenue targets, market share goals, or customer acquisition numbers. Clear objectives provide a benchmark for success and guide your sales strategy.

3. **Identify Your Unique Selling Proposition (USP):** Determine what sets your product or service apart from the competition. Your USP should highlight the unique benefits and value your offering provides to customers. This differentiation will help your sales team effectively communicate your product's advantages.
4. **Develop Sales Tactics:** Outline the tactics your sales team will use to achieve the defined objectives. This may include lead generation strategies, sales presentations, pricing models, and promotional offers. Ensure your tactics align with your market analysis and target audience.
5. **Allocate Resources:** Determine the resources needed to implement your sales strategy, including budget, personnel, and tools. Invest in the necessary resources to support your sales team and enable them to perform effectively.
6. **Monitor and Adjust:** Continuously monitor the progress of your sales strategy. Use key performance indicators (KPIs) to track

performance and make adjustments as needed. Be prepared to adapt your strategy based on changing market conditions and feedback from your sales team.

Sales Techniques and Skills

Sales techniques and skills are crucial for converting leads into customers and achieving sales goals. Here's a breakdown of essential techniques and skills for successful selling:

1. **Prospecting and Lead Generation:** Effective prospecting involves identifying potential customers and generating leads. Use methods such as networking, referrals, and social media to find and qualify leads. Develop a systematic approach to prospecting to maintain a steady pipeline of potential customers.

2. **Effective Communication:** Strong communication skills are essential for successful sales. This includes active listening, clear articulation of value propositions, and the ability to address customer concerns. Tailor your communication style to the needs and preferences of each customer.

3. **Sales Presentation:** A compelling sales presentation is key to engaging potential customers and closing deals. Focus on

demonstrating the benefits and value of your product, addressing customer pain points, and providing solutions. Use storytelling and visuals to make your presentation more impactful.

4. **Negotiation Skills:** Negotiation is a critical part of the sales process. Develop skills in negotiating terms, pricing, and contracts. Aim for win-win outcomes where both you and the customer feel satisfied with the agreement. Practice flexibility while maintaining the integrity of your value proposition.
5. **Closing Techniques:** Closing techniques are methods used to finalize a sale. Common techniques include the assumptive close (assuming the customer will buy), the urgency close (creating a sense of urgency), and the summary close (recapping benefits and asking for the sale). Choose the technique that best fits the customer's situation.
6. **Customer Relationship Management:** Building and maintaining strong customer relationships is essential for repeat business and referrals. Use customer relationship management (CRM) systems to track interactions, follow up on leads,

and manage customer information effectively.

Managing Sales Teams and Performance

Effective sales management involves leading and supporting your sales team to achieve their goals. Here's how to manage your sales team and enhance performance:

1. **Recruit and Train:** Hire individuals with the right skills and attitude for your sales team. Provide comprehensive training to ensure they understand your products, sales techniques, and company processes. Ongoing training and development will help them stay updated with industry trends and improve their skills.
2. **Set Clear Expectations:** Clearly communicate expectations and performance standards to your sales team. This includes setting sales targets, defining key performance metrics, and outlining responsibilities. Ensure that your team understands what is required to achieve success.
3. **Provide Support and Resources:** Offer support and resources to help your sales team succeed. This may include access to sales tools, marketing materials, and administrative support. Foster a supportive

environment where team members can seek help and share best practices.

4. **Monitor Performance:** Regularly assess the performance of your sales team using KPIs such as sales volume, conversion rates, and customer satisfaction. Use performance data to provide constructive feedback and identify areas for improvement.
5. **Motivate and Reward:** Implement motivation and reward programs to encourage high performance. Recognize and reward achievements such as meeting or exceeding sales targets, securing new clients, or demonstrating exceptional customer service. Motivation can drive enthusiasm and commitment.
6. **Foster Team Collaboration:** Promote a collaborative culture within your sales team. Encourage knowledge sharing, teamwork, and mutual support. Collaboration can lead to innovative solutions, improved performance, and a positive team dynamic.

Additional Points

- **Sales Forecasting:** Utilize sales forecasting techniques to predict future sales performance based on historical data and market trends. Accurate forecasting helps with resource allocation, budgeting, and strategic planning.

- **Customer Feedback:** Incorporate customer feedback into your sales strategy and team training. Understanding customer experiences and concerns can provide valuable insights for improving sales tactics and processes.
- **Sales Analytics:** Use sales analytics to gain insights into sales performance, customer behavior, and market trends. Analyze data to identify patterns, measure the effectiveness of sales strategies, and make informed decisions.
- **Adapting to Change:** Stay adaptable and responsive to changes in the market, customer preferences, and industry developments. Regularly review and update your sales strategy to remain competitive and address evolving challenges.

In conclusion, effective sales management is crucial for driving revenue and achieving business success. By building a solid sales strategy, mastering essential sales techniques and skills, and managing your sales team effectively, you can create a high-performing sales organization that meets your goals and exceeds customer expectations. As you continue to develop your sales management capabilities, remember that ongoing learning, adaptability, and a focus on customer needs are key to sustained success in the ever-evolving sales landscape.

Chapter 10: Customer Relationship Management

Welcome to Chapter 10, where we explore the critical field of Customer Relationship Management (CRM). CRM is not just a set of tools but a comprehensive strategy for building and maintaining strong relationships with customers. This chapter will delve into the importance of customer relationships, the tools and techniques for managing them, and strategies for enhancing customer satisfaction and loyalty.

Importance of Customer Relationships

Building and maintaining robust customer relationships is essential for long-term business success. Let's explore why these relationships are so crucial:

1. **Customer Retention:** Strong relationships lead to increased customer retention. When customers feel valued and supported, they are more likely to remain loyal to your brand. Retaining existing customers is often more cost-effective than acquiring new ones, making relationship management a key to sustainable growth.
2. **Repeat Business:** Satisfied customers are more likely to make repeat purchases. By fostering a positive relationship, you

encourage customers to return, thereby boosting your revenue and creating a stable customer base.

3. **Word-of-Mouth Referrals:** Happy customers are your best advocates. They are likely to recommend your product or service to friends and family, providing valuable word-of-mouth referrals. This organic promotion can significantly enhance your brand's reputation and attract new customers.
4. **Customer Feedback:** Strong relationships facilitate open communication, allowing you to gather valuable feedback. Understanding customer needs, preferences, and concerns helps you make informed decisions and improve your products and services.
5. **Competitive Advantage:** Excellent customer service and relationship management can differentiate you from competitors. In a crowded market, providing exceptional customer experiences can set your brand apart and build a loyal customer base.

Tools and Techniques for Managing Customer Relationships

Managing customer relationships effectively requires the right tools and techniques. Here's a guide to some essential CRM tools and methods:

1. **Customer Relationship Management (CRM) Software:** CRM software is a powerful tool for managing customer interactions and data. It helps you track customer information, manage leads, and automate processes. Popular CRM systems include Salesforce, HubSpot, and Zoho CRM. Choose a CRM platform that suits your business needs and integrates with your existing systems.
2. **Customer Segmentation:** Segmenting your customer base allows you to tailor your approach to different groups. By categorizing customers based on factors such as demographics, purchase history, and behavior, you can create personalized marketing strategies and offers that resonate with each segment.
3. **Email Marketing:** Email marketing is an effective way to stay in touch with customers and nurture relationships. Use email campaigns to share updates, promotions, and personalized content. Segment your email lists to target specific groups and track engagement metrics to optimize your campaigns.

4. **Customer Support Tools:** Tools such as help desks, chatbots, and support ticket systems facilitate efficient customer support. These tools enable you to respond quickly to customer inquiries, resolve issues, and provide assistance. Implementing a robust support system enhances the overall customer experience.
5. **Loyalty Programs:** Loyalty programs reward customers for their repeat business and encourage continued engagement. Offer incentives such as discounts, points, or exclusive offers to loyal customers. A well-designed loyalty program can boost retention and increase customer lifetime value.
6. **Social Media Monitoring:** Social media platforms are valuable channels for engaging with customers and monitoring their feedback. Use social media monitoring tools to track mentions of your brand, respond to comments, and address concerns. Engage with your audience through meaningful interactions and content.
7. **Customer Surveys and Feedback:** Regularly solicit feedback from customers through surveys and feedback forms. This helps you understand their experiences, identify

areas for improvement, and make data-driven decisions. Use feedback to enhance your products, services, and customer interactions.

Enhancing Customer Satisfaction and Loyalty

Enhancing customer satisfaction and loyalty requires a proactive approach and a commitment to delivering exceptional experiences. Here are strategies to achieve this:

1. **Personalization:** Personalize interactions and communications to make customers feel valued. Address customers by name, tailor recommendations based on their preferences, and provide relevant content. Personalization creates a more engaging and meaningful experience.

2. **Consistency:** Consistency in service and communication builds trust and reliability. Ensure that your brand's messaging, customer support, and overall experience are consistent across all touchpoints. Consistent experiences contribute to a positive brand perception.

3. **Exceptional Customer Service:** Provide outstanding customer service to exceed expectations. Train your staff to be knowledgeable, empathetic, and responsive. A helpful and friendly attitude

can turn a dissatisfied customer into a loyal advocate.

4. **Proactive Engagement:** Engage with customers proactively rather than waiting for them to reach out. Follow up after purchases, check in on their satisfaction, and offer assistance as needed. Proactive engagement demonstrates that you care about their experience and well-being.

5. **Addressing Issues Promptly:** Address customer issues and complaints promptly and effectively. Listen to their concerns, provide solutions, and ensure that problems are resolved to their satisfaction. A swift and effective response can turn a negative experience into a positive one.

6. **Building Emotional Connections:** Foster emotional connections with your customers by creating meaningful experiences and showing genuine care. Share stories, celebrate milestones, and engage with customers on a personal level. Emotional connections strengthen loyalty and enhance customer relationships.

Additional Points

- **Customer Journey Mapping:** Create a customer journey map to visualize and understand the entire customer experience from initial contact to post-purchase. This helps identify pain points and opportunities for improvement along the customer journey.

- **Data Security and Privacy:** Ensure that customer data is protected and handled with care. Implement robust data security measures and comply with privacy regulations. Building trust through data security enhances customer confidence and loyalty.
- **Continuous Improvement:** Regularly review and update your CRM strategies and tools. Stay informed about industry trends and emerging technologies that can enhance customer relationship management. Continuously seek ways to improve and adapt to changing customer expectations.
- **Empower Your Team:** Empower your team members to make decisions and take ownership of customer interactions. Provide training and resources to equip them with the skills needed to excel in managing customer relationships. A motivated and empowered team contributes to better customer experiences.

In conclusion, effective Customer Relationship Management is vital for building strong, lasting connections with your customers. By understanding the importance of customer relationships, utilizing the right tools and techniques, and implementing strategies to enhance satisfaction and loyalty, you can create a customer-centric approach that drives business success. Remember, building and maintaining positive relationships with your customers is an ongoing process that requires dedication, empathy, and continuous improvement. As you implement these strategies, keep the customer at the heart of your efforts and strive to exceed their expectations at every touchpoint.

Chapter 11: Marketing Metrics and Evaluation

Welcome to Chapter 11, where we explore the critical field of marketing metrics and evaluation. In today's data-driven world, measuring the effectiveness of your marketing efforts is essential for understanding what works, what doesn't, and how to optimize your strategies. This chapter will guide you through measuring marketing effectiveness, analyzing marketing metrics and Key Performance Indicators (KPIs), and making data-driven marketing decisions.

Measuring Marketing Effectiveness

Marketing effectiveness refers to how well your marketing activities achieve their intended goals. To measure effectiveness, you need to evaluate various aspects of your marketing efforts. Here's how you can do it:

1. **Define Clear Objectives:** Before measuring effectiveness, establish clear, specific objectives for your marketing campaigns. Objectives could include increasing brand awareness, generating leads, boosting sales, or improving customer engagement. Clear objectives provide a basis for measuring success.

2. **Identify Key Metrics:** Choose metrics that align with your objectives. For example, if your goal is to increase brand awareness, you might measure metrics such as website traffic, social media reach, and media mentions. If your goal is to boost sales, focus on metrics like conversion rates, sales revenue, and average order value.
3. **Use Tracking Tools:** Employ various tools to track and measure your marketing activities. Analytics platforms like Google Analytics, social media insights, and email marketing software provide data on campaign performance. Set up tracking codes and tags to capture relevant data accurately.
4. **Monitor Campaign Performance:** Continuously monitor the performance of your marketing campaigns. Track metrics in real-time to identify trends and assess whether you're on track to achieve your objectives. Regular monitoring allows you to make timely adjustments if needed.
5. **Evaluate ROI:** Calculate the Return on Investment (ROI) for your marketing efforts. ROI measures the profitability of your campaigns by comparing the revenue generated to the costs incurred. A positive

ROI indicates that your marketing investments are yielding returns.

Analyzing Marketing Metrics and KPIs

Analyzing marketing metrics and KPIs (Key Performance Indicators) helps you gain insights into your marketing performance and identify areas for improvement. Here's how to effectively analyze these metrics:

1. **Segment Your Data:** Break down your data into segments to gain deeper insights. For example, analyze metrics by demographics, geography, or traffic sources. Segmentation helps you understand which segments perform better and tailor your strategies accordingly.

2. **Compare Against Benchmarks:** Compare your metrics to industry benchmarks or historical data. Benchmarks provide a standard for evaluating performance and help you determine whether your results are above or below average. Use this comparison to set realistic goals and expectations.

3. **Identify Trends and Patterns:** Look for trends and patterns in your data. Analyzing trends over time can reveal seasonal effects, shifts in customer behavior, or the impact of specific campaigns.

Understanding these patterns helps you make informed decisions and plan future strategies.

4. **Perform A/B Testing:** Conduct A/B testing to compare the performance of different marketing approaches. Test variations of ads, emails, or landing pages to see which performs better. Analyzing the results of these tests provides valuable insights into what resonates with your audience.

5. **Evaluate Customer Behavior:** Analyze metrics related to customer behavior, such as click-through rates, bounce rates, and time spent on your site. Understanding how customers interact with your marketing materials helps you optimize content and improve engagement.

6. **Track Conversion Metrics:** Monitor conversion metrics to assess how well your marketing efforts drive desired actions. Track metrics such as conversion rates, cost per conversion, and customer acquisition cost. Evaluating these metrics helps you understand the effectiveness of your lead generation and sales strategies.

Making Data-Driven Marketing Decisions

Data-driven decision-making involves using data insights to guide your marketing strategies and actions. Here's how to make informed decisions based on your analysis:

1. **Set Data-Driven Goals:** Base your marketing goals on data insights rather than assumptions. Use historical data and market research to set realistic and achievable goals. Data-driven goals provide a solid foundation for planning and measuring success.

2. **Leverage Insights for Strategy:** Use the insights gained from your analysis to inform your marketing strategy. For example, if data reveals that a particular audience segment responds well to certain content, tailor your strategy to focus on that segment and content type.

3. **Optimize Campaigns Continuously:** Use data to optimize your marketing campaigns in real-time. Make adjustments to targeting, messaging, and channels based on performance data. Continuous optimization ensures that you're making the most of your marketing efforts.

4. **Allocate Resources Wisely:** Allocate your marketing resources based on performance data. Invest more in high-performing channels and strategies while scaling back on underperforming ones. Data-driven

resource allocation maximizes the effectiveness of your budget.

5. **Communicate Findings:** Share data insights and findings with your team and stakeholders. Clear communication ensures that everyone understands the rationale behind marketing decisions and fosters a collaborative approach to strategy development.

6. **Learn from Successes and Failures:** Analyze both successful and unsuccessful campaigns to learn from your experiences. Identify what worked well and what didn't, and apply these lessons to future strategies. Embracing a learning mindset helps you continuously improve.

Additional Points

- **Data Privacy and Ethics:** Ensure that your data collection and analysis practices comply with data privacy regulations and ethical standards. Respect customer privacy and handle data responsibly to build trust and avoid legal issues.

- **Integrate Data Sources:** Integrate data from various sources to gain a comprehensive view of your marketing performance. Combining data from CRM systems, social media, and email marketing provides a holistic understanding of your campaigns.

- **Invest in Data Analytics Tools:** Consider investing in advanced data analytics tools and platforms that offer deeper insights and predictive analytics. Tools such as Google Analytics 4, Tableau, and Adobe Analytics provide enhanced capabilities for data analysis.
- **Foster a Data-Driven Culture:** Encourage a data-driven culture within your organization. Promote the use of data and analytics in decision-making across all departments. A data-driven culture enhances overall business performance and adaptability.

In conclusion, marketing metrics and evaluation are vital for understanding the effectiveness of your marketing efforts and making informed decisions. By measuring marketing effectiveness, analyzing metrics and KPIs, and leveraging data-driven insights, you can optimize your strategies, achieve your objectives, and drive business success. Remember, effective marketing management is a continuous process of monitoring, analyzing, and adapting based on data. Embrace data-driven decision-making as a fundamental part of your marketing approach to stay competitive and responsive in a dynamic market environment.

Chapter 12: Ethical and Legal Considerations in Marketing

Welcome to Chapter 12, where we tackle the important topics of ethical and legal considerations in marketing. In today's complex business environment, navigating ethical dilemmas and legal regulations is crucial for maintaining a reputable and compliant marketing practice. This chapter will cover the essentials of marketing ethics, the legal regulations you need to be aware of, and how to build ethical marketing practices.

Understanding Marketing Ethics

Marketing ethics refers to the moral principles and standards that guide marketing practices. It involves making decisions that align with ethical values and ensuring that marketing activities do not deceive or harm consumers. Here's a deeper look at key aspects of marketing ethics:

1. **Honesty and Transparency:** One of the fundamental ethical principles in marketing is honesty. Ensure that all marketing communications are truthful and transparent. Avoid making exaggerated claims or misleading statements about your products or services. Being honest builds trust with your

audience and maintains your brand's integrity.

2. **Respect for Privacy:** Respecting customer privacy is a critical ethical consideration. Ensure that you handle customer data responsibly and obtain consent before collecting personal information. Use data only for the purposes for which it was collected and protect it from unauthorized access or misuse.
3. **Fairness and Equity:** Marketing practices should be fair and equitable, avoiding exploitation or discrimination. Ensure that your marketing efforts do not unfairly target vulnerable populations or perpetuate stereotypes. Aim to create marketing campaigns that are inclusive and respectful to all individuals.
4. **Social Responsibility:** Consider the broader impact of your marketing activities on society. Avoid promoting harmful products or practices, and support initiatives that contribute positively to social well-being. Socially responsible marketing can enhance your brand's reputation and align with consumer values.
5. **Ethical Influences:** Be mindful of the ethical implications of your marketing

strategies. For example, using psychological tactics to manipulate consumer behavior can be unethical. Strive to influence consumers through positive and honest means rather than through coercion or deceit.

Navigating Legal Regulations and Compliance

Legal regulations play a crucial role in guiding marketing practices and ensuring compliance with the law. Here's an overview of key legal considerations and how to navigate them:

1. **Advertising Standards:** Familiarize yourself with advertising regulations that govern how products and services can be promoted. Regulations may include rules on truthfulness, non-deceptive advertising, and the prohibition of false claims. In many countries, regulatory bodies such as the Federal Trade Commission (FTC) in the U.S. oversee advertising practices.

2. **Consumer Protection Laws:** Ensure that your marketing practices comply with consumer protection laws designed to safeguard consumers from unfair or deceptive practices. These laws cover areas such as false advertising, warranties, and product safety. Understanding and

adhering to these laws helps protect both consumers and your business.

3. **Data Protection Regulations:** Compliance with data protection regulations is essential for handling customer data responsibly. Regulations such as the General Data Protection Regulation (GDPR) in Europe and the California Consumer Privacy Act (CCPA) in the U.S. govern how businesses collect, store, and use personal information. Ensure that your marketing activities align with these regulations to avoid legal repercussions.

4. **Intellectual Property Laws:** Be aware of intellectual property laws that protect brand assets, including trademarks, copyrights, and patents. Avoid infringing on the intellectual property rights of others by using copyrighted materials or logos without permission. Respecting intellectual property rights fosters a fair competitive environment.

5. **Social Media Regulations:** Social media platforms have their own set of guidelines and regulations. Ensure that your marketing activities on social media comply with platform policies, including rules on advertising, sponsored content, and user privacy. Violating social media

regulations can result in penalties or account suspension.

Building Ethical Marketing Practices

Building ethical marketing practices involves integrating ethical considerations into every aspect of your marketing strategy. Here's how to create and maintain an ethical marketing approach:

1. **Develop an Ethical Marketing Policy:** Create a comprehensive ethical marketing policy that outlines your commitment to ethical practices. Include guidelines on honesty, transparency, privacy, and social responsibility. Ensure that all team members are aware of and adhere to this policy.
2. **Train Your Team:** Provide training on ethical marketing practices to your marketing team. Educate them about ethical principles, legal regulations, and the importance of integrity in marketing. Regular training helps ensure that everyone understands and follows ethical guidelines.
3. **Conduct Ethical Reviews:** Regularly review and assess your marketing campaigns to ensure they align with ethical standards. Conduct internal audits to identify

potential ethical issues and address them proactively. Implement feedback mechanisms to continuously improve your practices.

4. **Encourage Ethical Decision-Making:** Foster a culture of ethical decision-making within your organization. Encourage team members to raise ethical concerns and provide a safe environment for discussing ethical dilemmas. Support ethical behavior and recognize efforts to uphold ethical standards.

5. **Engage with Stakeholders:** Engage with stakeholders, including customers, employees, and community members, to understand their expectations and concerns regarding ethical marketing. Incorporate their feedback into your marketing practices and demonstrate your commitment to ethical conduct.

6. **Monitor and Adapt:** Stay informed about emerging ethical issues and evolving legal regulations in marketing. Monitor industry trends and adapt your practices as needed to address new challenges and opportunities. Being proactive ensures that your marketing remains ethical and compliant.

Additional Points

- **Ethical Marketing Certification:** Consider obtaining certification from organizations that promote ethical marketing practices. Certification can enhance your credibility and demonstrate your commitment to ethical standards.
- **Ethics in Crisis Management:** Develop strategies for handling ethical dilemmas during a crisis. Having a plan in place ensures that you can navigate challenges with integrity and maintain public trust.
- **Transparency in Influencer Marketing:** If using influencers, ensure that they disclose sponsored content and comply with advertising guidelines. Transparency in influencer marketing builds trust with your audience and maintains ethical standards.
- **Consumer Advocacy:** Support consumer advocacy initiatives that promote ethical business practices. Engaging with organizations that advocate for consumer rights can enhance your brand's reputation and align with ethical values.

In conclusion, navigating ethical and legal considerations in marketing is essential for building trust, maintaining compliance, and fostering a positive brand image. By understanding marketing ethics, adhering to legal regulations, and implementing ethical practices, you create a marketing environment that respects consumers and upholds integrity. Embrace ethical decision-making as a fundamental aspect of your marketing strategy and continuously strive to align your practices with ethical and legal standards. As you build and maintain ethical marketing practices, you not only enhance your brand's reputation but also contribute positively to the broader business and consumer community.

Chapter 13: Emerging Trends in Marketing

Welcome to Chapter 13, where we explore the exciting world of emerging trends in marketing. As technology evolves and consumer behaviors shift, the marketing landscape is constantly changing. In this chapter, we'll examine key innovations and technological advancements, envision the future of marketing, and discuss how to adapt to changing market dynamics.

Innovations and Technological Advancements

1. **Artificial Intelligence (AI) and Machine Learning:** AI and machine learning are revolutionizing marketing by enabling more personalized and data-driven approaches. AI algorithms analyze vast amounts of data to identify patterns and predict consumer behavior. This allows marketers to create highly targeted campaigns, optimize customer interactions, and improve decision-making. For example, AI-powered chatbots provide real-time customer support, while machine learning algorithms personalize product recommendations based on user behavior.
2. **Big Data and Analytics:** The rise of big data has transformed how marketers collect and

analyze information. With access to vast amounts of data from various sources, marketers can gain deep insights into consumer preferences, market trends, and campaign performance. Advanced analytics tools help in interpreting this data, enabling marketers to make informed decisions and develop strategies that drive better results.

3. **Augmented Reality (AR) and Virtual Reality (VR):** AR and VR technologies are enhancing customer experiences by creating immersive and interactive environments. AR allows users to visualize products in their real-world context, such as trying on virtual clothes or seeing how furniture fits in their home. VR provides fully immersive experiences, such as virtual tours or product demonstrations. These technologies engage customers in new and exciting ways, driving higher engagement and conversion rates.

4. **Voice Search and Voice Assistants:** The growing popularity of voice-activated devices, like Amazon's Alexa and Google Assistant, is changing how people search for information and interact with brands. Optimizing for voice search involves focusing on conversational keywords and

providing concise, relevant answers. Brands that adapt to this trend can enhance their visibility and accessibility in voice search results.

5. **Blockchain Technology:** Blockchain technology is enhancing transparency and security in digital marketing. It provides a decentralized and immutable ledger that can verify transactions, track ad impressions, and prevent ad fraud. By leveraging blockchain, marketers can ensure the authenticity of their data and build trust with consumers.
6. **Influencer Marketing Evolution:** Influencer marketing continues to evolve as brands seek more authentic and relatable voices to promote their products. Micro-influencers, who have smaller but highly engaged audiences, are becoming increasingly valuable. They often offer more targeted reach and higher engagement rates compared to traditional celebrities.

The Future of Marketing

1. **Hyper-Personalization:** The future of marketing will see an increased emphasis on hyper-personalization. With advancements in data analytics and AI,

marketers can create highly customized experiences for individual consumers. This includes personalized content, product recommendations, and targeted messaging based on detailed consumer profiles and behavior.

2. **Sustainability and Ethical Marketing:** Consumers are becoming more environmentally and socially conscious. Brands that prioritize sustainability and ethical practices will gain a competitive edge. Future marketing strategies will likely focus on promoting eco-friendly products, transparent supply chains, and corporate social responsibility initiatives.

3. **Experiential Marketing:** The future will see a greater emphasis on experiential marketing, where brands create memorable and interactive experiences for their customers. This approach goes beyond traditional advertising by engaging consumers in immersive brand experiences that foster emotional connections and brand loyalty.

4. **AI-Driven Creativity:** AI will not only enhance data analysis but also contribute to creative processes. AI tools can generate content ideas, design visuals, and even write copy. As AI becomes more

sophisticated, it will play a significant role in creative marketing, enabling faster and more innovative content creation.

5. **Omnichannel Marketing Integration:** The future of marketing will involve seamless integration across multiple channels. Consumers expect a consistent experience whether they interact with a brand online, in-store, or through mobile apps. Brands that successfully integrate their marketing efforts across channels will provide a more cohesive and satisfying customer experience.
6. **5G Technology:** The rollout of 5G technology will accelerate the delivery of high-speed, high-quality content. Marketers will be able to leverage 5G's capabilities to enhance mobile experiences, enable real-time interactions, and support data-intensive applications like AR and VR.

Adapting to Changing Market Dynamics

1. **Embrace Agility:** To stay competitive, marketers must embrace agility and be prepared to adapt to changing market dynamics. This involves being responsive to emerging trends, consumer preferences, and technological advancements. Agile marketing practices enable quick

adjustments and innovations to meet evolving demands.

2. **Continuous Learning:** Stay informed about the latest trends and developments in marketing. Regularly update your skills and knowledge through industry conferences, webinars, and online courses. Continuous learning helps you stay ahead of the curve and implement cutting-edge strategies.
3. **Leverage Data Insights:** Use data insights to drive decision-making and strategy development. Analyze market trends, consumer behavior, and campaign performance to identify opportunities and address challenges. Data-driven insights provide a solid foundation for adapting your marketing approach.
4. **Foster Innovation:** Encourage a culture of innovation within your marketing team. Experiment with new technologies, creative ideas, and unconventional strategies. Foster an environment where team members feel empowered to explore new possibilities and contribute to innovative marketing solutions.
5. **Build Strong Partnerships:** Collaborate with technology providers, influencers, and industry experts to enhance your

marketing efforts. Building strong partnerships can provide access to new tools, resources, and insights that support your adaptation to changing market dynamics.

6. **Focus on Customer Experience:** Prioritize delivering exceptional customer experiences across all touchpoints. By understanding and addressing customer needs and preferences, you can build stronger relationships, enhance satisfaction, and drive loyalty.

Additional Points

- **Ethical Considerations with Emerging Technologies:** As you adopt new technologies, consider the ethical implications of their use. Ensure that technologies like AI and data analytics are used responsibly and transparently, respecting consumer privacy and avoiding biases.

- **Adaptation in Crisis Situations:** Be prepared to adapt your marketing strategies in response to crisis situations, such as economic downturns or global events. Flexibility and resilience are key to navigating uncertain times and maintaining brand relevance.

- **Consumer-Centric Approach:** Focus on understanding and addressing consumer needs and preferences. A consumer-centric approach helps you tailor your marketing efforts to meet evolving demands and build stronger connections with your audience.

In conclusion, emerging trends in marketing offer exciting opportunities and challenges. By embracing innovations and technological advancements, preparing for the future of marketing, and adapting to changing market dynamics, you can stay ahead in a rapidly evolving landscape. Embrace these trends with an open mind, continuously learn and innovate, and remain focused on delivering exceptional experiences to your customers. As you navigate the future of marketing, your adaptability and forward-thinking approach will be key to achieving success in this dynamic field.

Chapter 14: Case Studies and Real-World Applications

Welcome to Chapter 14, where we delve into the practical side of marketing through case studies and real-world applications. Understanding both successful and failed marketing campaigns provides valuable insights into what works, what doesn't, and why. By examining these examples, you can gain practical knowledge and lessons that will enhance your marketing strategies.

Analyzing Successful Marketing Campaigns

1. **Coca-Cola's "Share a Coke" Campaign:** Coca-Cola's "Share a Coke" campaign is a prime example of a successful marketing initiative. Launched in Australia in 2011 and expanded globally, this campaign replaced the Coca-Cola logo on bottles with popular names and terms of endearment. The campaign created a personal connection with consumers, encouraging them to find bottles with their names or the names of loved ones. This personalized approach led to a significant increase in sales and brand engagement. The success of the campaign highlights the power of personalization and the impact of creating emotional connections with customers.

2. **Apple's "Think Different" Campaign:** Apple's "Think Different" campaign, launched in 1997, is a classic example of successful brand positioning. The campaign celebrated individuals who changed the world through their creativity and innovation. By aligning the Apple brand with iconic figures like Albert Einstein and Martin Luther King Jr., the campaign reinforced Apple's identity as a revolutionary and creative company. This strategy helped Apple differentiate itself from competitors and build a strong brand image. The campaign's success demonstrates the importance of aligning marketing messages with a brand's core values and vision.

3. **Nike's "Just Do It" Campaign:** Nike's "Just Do It" campaign, introduced in 1988, is another exemplary case of effective marketing. The slogan, paired with motivational imagery and endorsements from athletes, resonated with consumers and became a powerful symbol of empowerment and perseverance. The campaign's success is attributed to its ability to inspire and connect with a wide audience on an emotional level. It also showcases the effectiveness of a strong, memorable slogan in building brand

identity and driving consumer engagement.

Learning from Marketing Failures

1. **Pepsi's "Kendall Jenner Ad":** Pepsi's 2017 advertisement featuring Kendall Jenner faced significant backlash for appearing to trivialize social justice movements. The ad, which depicted Jenner resolving a protest by handing a police officer a Pepsi, was criticized for its insensitivity and lack of understanding of social issues. The backlash led to Pepsi pulling the ad and issuing an apology. This failure highlights the importance of being mindful of social and cultural contexts in marketing. Brands must approach sensitive topics with genuine respect and understanding to avoid appearing exploitative.

2. **New Coke:** In 1985, Coca-Cola introduced "New Coke" with a reformulated taste. The change was met with strong resistance from consumers who preferred the original formula. The backlash was so intense that Coca-Cola eventually reintroduced the original formula as "Coca-Cola Classic." This failure underscores the risks of altering a beloved product and the importance of understanding consumer preferences. It also illustrates the value of

maintaining a strong connection with customer expectations and brand loyalty.

3. **Gap's Logo Redesign:** In 2010, Gap unveiled a new logo as part of a rebranding effort, but it was met with immediate criticism from customers who preferred the old logo. The negative feedback was so overwhelming that Gap reverted to the original logo within a week. This case highlights the importance of involving customers in rebranding efforts and understanding the emotional attachment they may have to a brand's visual identity.

Practical Applications and Lessons Learned

1. **Customer-Centric Approach:** Both successful and failed campaigns emphasize the importance of understanding and catering to customer needs and preferences. Successful campaigns often involve a deep understanding of the target audience and their desires. Regularly gather feedback and conduct market research to ensure your marketing strategies align with consumer expectations.
2. **Personalization Matters:** Personalization can significantly enhance the effectiveness of marketing campaigns. Tailoring

messages and offers to individual preferences creates a stronger connection with consumers and increases engagement. Implement data-driven personalization strategies to make your marketing efforts more relevant and impactful.

3. **Cultural Sensitivity:** Be aware of cultural and social contexts when designing marketing campaigns. Sensitivity to cultural differences and current social issues is crucial to avoid missteps and backlash. Engage with diverse perspectives and conduct thorough research to ensure your marketing messages resonate positively with your audience.

4. **Innovation and Adaptability:** The ability to innovate and adapt to changing market conditions is vital for success. Learn from both successes and failures to refine your strategies and stay relevant. Embrace new technologies and trends while being mindful of their potential impact on your audience and brand.

5. **Effective Communication:** Clear and transparent communication is essential in both marketing and crisis management. Ensure that your messaging is consistent, honest, and aligned with your brand values. In the event of a failure or controversy,

address the issue promptly and take responsibility to maintain consumer trust.

6. **Test and Iterate:** Before launching a full-scale campaign, test your ideas on a smaller scale to gather insights and identify potential issues. Use pilot programs, A/B testing, and focus groups to refine your strategies and improve their effectiveness. Iteration based on real-world feedback helps in optimizing your campaigns for better results.

Additional Points

- **Consumer Engagement:** Actively engage with your audience through social media, surveys, and feedback mechanisms. Building strong relationships with consumers can provide valuable insights and foster loyalty.
- **Ethical Considerations:** Incorporate ethical considerations into your marketing practices. Ensure that your campaigns promote positive values and respect consumer rights.
- **Competitive Analysis:** Analyze the successes and failures of competitors to gain insights into industry trends and best practices. Use this knowledge to refine your

own strategies and differentiate your brand.

In conclusion, studying case studies of successful and failed marketing campaigns provides valuable lessons that can inform your marketing strategies. By analyzing these real-world examples, you can gain practical insights into what works, what doesn't, and why. Apply these lessons to your own marketing efforts, and strive to create campaigns that resonate with your audience, adapt to changing dynamics, and uphold ethical standards. Learning from both successes and failures equips you with the knowledge and skills to navigate the ever-evolving landscape of marketing effectively.

Conclusion

As we wrap up this comprehensive exploration of business marketing, it's essential to reflect on the key takeaways, consider future directions, and offer final thoughts to guide you on your marketing journey. Let's summarize what we've learned and look ahead to the exciting possibilities in the field of marketing.

Summarizing Key Takeaways

1. **The Core of Marketing:** At its heart, marketing is about understanding and meeting consumer needs. From developing a solid marketing strategy to implementing effective promotional tactics, everything revolves around connecting with your target audience and delivering value. We've explored the importance of market research, consumer behavior, and strategic planning in crafting successful marketing initiatives.

2. **The Power of Innovation:** Innovation is a driving force in marketing. Embracing technological advancements like AI, big data, and AR/VR can significantly enhance your marketing efforts. Staying ahead of trends and adapting to new tools and techniques is crucial for maintaining a

competitive edge and engaging your audience effectively.

3. **Learning from Real-World Examples:** Case studies of successful and failed campaigns offer valuable lessons. Understanding what worked and what didn't provides insights into effective strategies and potential pitfalls. Applying these lessons to your own marketing efforts can help you refine your approach and avoid common mistakes.
4. **Ethics and Responsibility:** Ethical considerations are fundamental in marketing. Building trust with consumers requires transparency, respect, and responsibility. Navigating legal regulations and fostering ethical practices are essential for maintaining a positive brand reputation and ensuring long-term success.
5. **Customer-Centric Approach:** The importance of focusing on the customer cannot be overstated. Personalization, engagement, and responsiveness are key to creating meaningful connections and driving loyalty. By understanding and addressing customer needs, you can build stronger relationships and enhance your marketing impact.

Future Directions in Business Marketing

1. **Increased Personalization:** As technology continues to evolve, the potential for hyper-personalization will grow. Leveraging advanced data analytics and AI, marketers will be able to create even more tailored and relevant experiences for individual consumers. Expect to see more sophisticated approaches to personalization that enhance customer satisfaction and drive engagement.

2. **Sustainability and Social Responsibility:** The future of marketing will see a stronger emphasis on sustainability and social responsibility. Consumers are increasingly valuing brands that demonstrate a commitment to environmental and social issues. Incorporating sustainable practices and promoting ethical values will become more integral to marketing strategies.

3. **Integration of Emerging Technologies:** The integration of emerging technologies such as 5G, blockchain, and advanced AI will shape the future of marketing. These technologies will enable new ways to connect with consumers, optimize marketing efforts, and enhance the overall customer experience. Staying informed and adaptable will be crucial for leveraging these innovations effectively.

4. **Evolution of Consumer Behavior:** Consumer behavior will continue to evolve with changing societal trends and technological advancements. Marketers must remain agile and responsive to these changes, continually adjusting their strategies to meet shifting preferences and expectations.
5. **Enhanced Data Utilization:** The use of data will become even more sophisticated, with advanced analytics and machine learning providing deeper insights into consumer behavior and market trends. Marketers will need to harness these data-driven insights to make informed decisions and drive strategic initiatives.

Final Thoughts and Encouragement for Marketers

Marketing is a dynamic and ever-evolving field that offers endless opportunities for creativity and innovation. As you navigate this landscape, keep the following thoughts in mind:

- **Embrace Change:** The marketing world is constantly changing. Embrace new trends, technologies, and approaches with an open mind. Being adaptable and willing to experiment will help you stay ahead and discover new opportunities.

- **Focus on the Customer:** Always keep the customer at the center of your strategies. Understanding their needs, preferences, and behaviors will guide your marketing efforts and ensure that you deliver meaningful and valuable experiences.
- **Learn Continuously:** Marketing is a field where continuous learning is essential. Stay informed about industry developments, seek out new knowledge, and apply what you learn to enhance your marketing practices.
- **Be Ethical and Responsible:** Uphold ethical standards and prioritize transparency and integrity in your marketing efforts. Building trust with consumers is fundamental to long-term success.
- **Innovate and Inspire:** Don't be afraid to push boundaries and think outside the box. Innovation and creativity are key drivers of successful marketing. Inspire your audience with fresh ideas and impactful campaigns.

In closing, the journey through business marketing is both challenging and rewarding. By applying the insights and lessons from this book, you can craft effective strategies, connect with your audience, and drive meaningful results.

Keep exploring, learning, and evolving in your marketing practice, and remember that the future of marketing is full of exciting possibilities. Good luck, and may your marketing endeavors be both impactful and fulfilling.

Epilogue

As we conclude "Business Marketing," it is clear that the principles and practices of marketing are integral to the success of any business. Throughout this book, we've explored a range of topics, from market research and consumer behavior to strategic planning and emerging trends.

The key takeaways from our journey highlight the importance of adaptability, customer focus, and innovation in marketing. As you move forward, remember that the marketing landscape will continue to evolve, and staying informed and adaptable will be crucial to your success.

Marketing is not just about promoting products or services—it's about creating meaningful connections with your audience and delivering value. By applying the strategies and insights shared in this book, you can craft effective marketing campaigns, build strong brand identities, and achieve your business objectives.

Thank you for joining me in this exploration of business marketing. I hope this book has provided you with valuable knowledge and inspiration to drive your marketing efforts and achieve success in your endeavors.

Author's Note

Dear Readers,

Thank you for taking the time to read "Business Marketing." Writing this book has been a rewarding journey, and I am grateful for the opportunity to share my knowledge and experiences with you.

Marketing is a dynamic field, and staying ahead requires continuous learning and adaptation. I hope that the insights and strategies presented in this book will serve as a valuable resource for you, whether you are just starting out in marketing or looking to refine your existing strategies.

If you have any questions, feedback, or would like to share your experiences, I would love to hear from you. Your thoughts and perspectives are invaluable and can help shape future editions of this book.

Wishing you all the best in your marketing endeavors.

Sincerely,

Andleeb Kamal

Thank You Letter to Publication

Dear Gyanvriksha Publications Team,

I am writing to extend my heartfelt gratitude for your support and collaboration in publishing "Business Marketing." Your dedication and professionalism have been instrumental in bringing this project to fruition, and I am truly appreciative of the effort and care you have put into this book.

Working with you has been a rewarding experience, and I am impressed by your commitment to excellence. The quality of the final product reflects the hard work and passion of your team, and I am proud to have partnered with such a reputable publication.

Thank you once again for your invaluable support. I look forward to future opportunities to work together and contribute to the world of business marketing.

Best regards,

Andleeb Kamal

9 789395 083997

Printed at Repro India Ltd.